A Nature's Footprint Guide

ANIMAL
FOOTNOTES

By Q. L. Pearce

Illustrated by Delana Bettoli

Silver Press

For my mother,
Doreen
−Q.L.P.

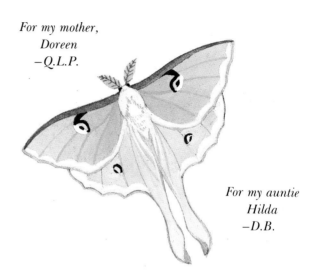

For my auntie
Hilda
−D.B.

With special thanks to Susan Poskanzer
for her editorial guidance.

10 9 8 7 6 5 4 3 2 1

Library of Congress Cataloging-in-Publication Data

Pearce, Q.L. (Querida Lee)
    Animal footnotes / written by Q.L. Pearce : illustrated by Delana Bettoli.
      p.   cm.
    Summary: Presents visual and textual information about various animals and their tracks or footprints, arranged alphabetically from antelope to Zebra.
    1. Animal tracks—Dictionaries, Juvenile.   2. Animals—Juvenile Literature. [1. Animal tracks—Dictionaries. 2. Animals—Dictionaries.] I. Bettoli, Delana, ill. II. Title.
QL768.P43   1990   89-70203
591—dc20   CIP
                                             AC
ISBN 0-671-69117-1   ISBN0-671-69116-3 (lib. bdg.)

A Note to Parents

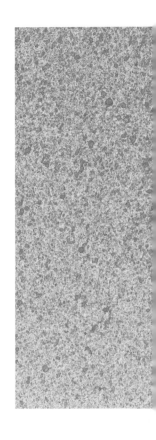

ANIMAL FOOTNOTES can be a valuable tool in helping children to understand and enjoy the world of animals. From antelopes to zebras, this book focuses on animal locomotion. Your child will see footprints of forty animals and learn facts about their feet, speed, and travel habits in a fun, interactive way. Children will also discover information about animal habits and habitats, diets and defenses. You may wish to have a globe or an atlas nearby to point out specific locations. Examining the introductory pages about animal classes before exploring the book may also be helpful.

The information in ANIMAL FOOTNOTES will be enhanced by using its companion series, the NATURE'S FOOTPRINTS "read aloud" picture books.

How to Use ANIMAL FOOTNOTES

ANIMAL FOOTNOTES is filled with notes about many different kinds of animals. But you will find yourself learning facts with a new twist. This book tells how animals move. You'll track footprints. You'll learn how and where animals travel and how fast they can go. You'll find out about animal feet. And you'll see how some animals move without any feet at all!

You may want to try moving the way the animals do. Can you crawl with your arms and legs sticking straight out? A Gila monster does. Can you run on two toes? An ostrich can. This book will give you many new ideas to try out.

You'll also learn about each animal's habitat. Habitat is the kind of place in which an animal lives. For example, the desert is the habitat of that quick little bird, the roadrunner. You will discover how an animal protects itself in its habitat and what it eats there.

You'll find that some animals are alike in certain ways. These animals belong to the same class. For example, animals that have feathers and beaks are in the class we call birds. The next twelve pages of the book tell about six animal classes. Special pages at the back of the book let you follow footprints to find hidden animals.

In between, you will find facts about forty different animals. They are listed in alphabetical order. This means that animal names beginning with A come first. These are followed by those beginning with B, then C, all the way to Z for zebra. Listing the names this way will help you easily find particular animals. Do you HAVE to read them in this order? Absolutely not. Take a minute to flip through the book. Find your favorite animals. Then go on to read about others you don't know as well.

You may find yourself noticing animal footprints around your home. The best time to find them is often the morning after a light rain. Take this book outside with you. Let it help you identify the prints. You may be surprised at how much you know about nature's footprints!

AMPHIBIANS

Amphibians (am-FIB-ee-enz) were the first animals with backbones to live on land. They are cold-blooded. Their bodies remain at the temperature of the water or air around them. On a cold day, an amphibian's body will be just as cold as the air or water.

Most amphibians live part of their lives in water and part on land. They start in the water. For example, a baby frog is a tadpole. A tadpole looks, acts, and breathes more like a fish than a frog. Later it grows legs and crawls onto land. It breathes air through lungs as we do. It also breathes through its moist, scaleless skin.

Adult amphibians usually live near water. They lay their eggs near or in wet places so they won't dry out.

The frogs, toad, and salamander on these pages are amphibians. Most salamanders have four legs and a long tail. Frogs usually have longer legs than toads. Look at the legs of the spade foot toad and the arrow poison frog. Which one has longer legs?

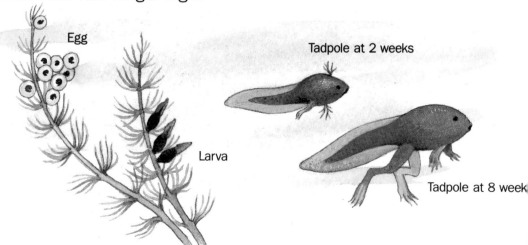

Egg

Larva

Tadpole at 2 weeks

Tadpole at 8 week

Arrow Poison Frog

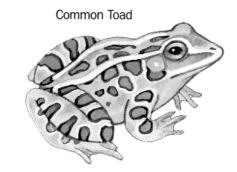

Common Toad

Spadefoot Toad

Salamander

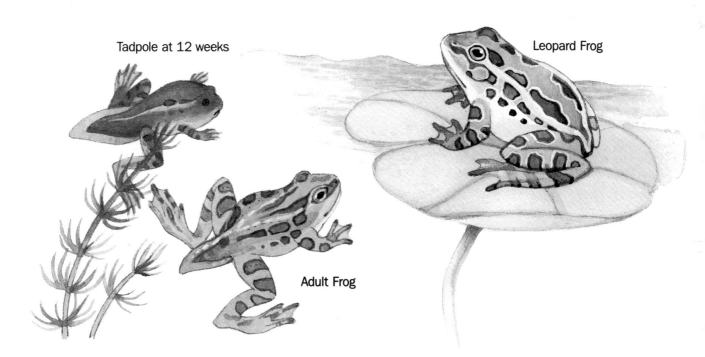

Tadpole at 12 weeks

Adult Frog

Leopard Frog

BIRDS

All birds have backbones. And they are warm-blooded. This means their body temperature always stays the same. On a hot day, a bird's body temperature is the same as on a cold day.

A baby bird hatches from a hard-shelled egg laid by its mother. Many birds build nests to protect their eggs. Some nests are made of sticks or grass. A few birds build nests of mud. Many line the nests with their own soft feathers. Birds are the only animals with feathers. Notice the different kinds of nests shown in the pictures.

Birds are the fastest-moving animals. Some can fly over 100 miles per hour. They all have wings. But not all birds can fly. An ostrich is too big and heavy to fly. Instead, it walks and runs. Some birds, like the hummingbird, can't walk or hop. They must fly wherever they want to go.

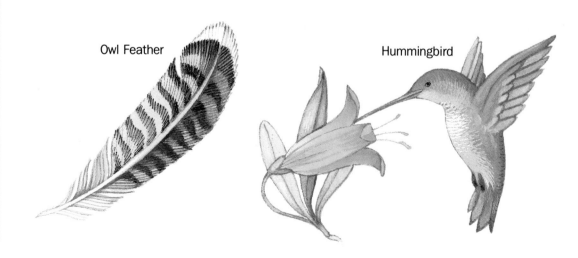

Owl Feather

Hummingbird

Bald Eagle

Red-winged
Blackbird

Barn Swallow

Male Ostrich

Albatross

Penguin

FISH

A little goldfish in a bowl and a mighty shark in the sea may seem very different. But they are both fish. All fish are cold-blooded and have backbones. Fish live in the water their whole lives. They have gills that let them breathe in the water. To get air, fish gulp water. Then they force the water over their gills. The gills take air from the water.

Fish swim using sail-like parts called fins. And most fish are streamlined. Their sleek shape helps them move quickly through the water. The tuna is one such fish. Many fish that live on the bottom of a lake or sea are flat. The flounder is a flat fish. In fact, both eyes are on one side of its head. Check the flounder in the picture. Imagine how it sees things.

Fish sleep. But they have no eyelids to close. When they sleep, they keep moving their fins. This helps them stay in the same place in the water. Then they know where they are when they wake up!

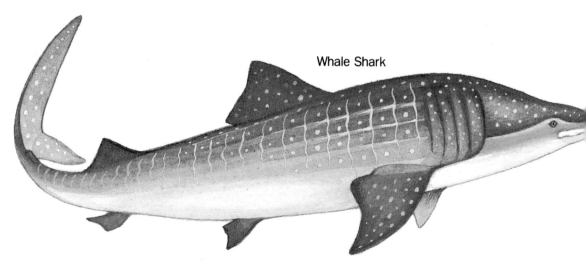

Whale Shark

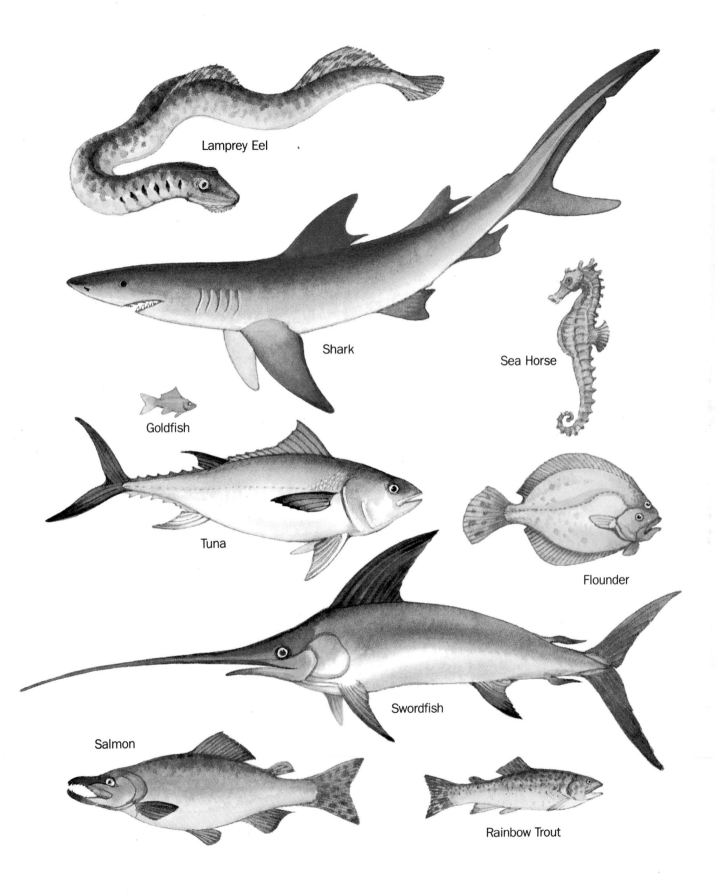

Lamprey Eel

Shark

Sea Horse

Goldfish

Tuna

Flounder

Swordfish

Salmon

Rainbow Trout

INSECTS

Insects were the first animals to live on land. An insect has no backbone. In fact, it has no bones at all! Instead, it has a hard covering called an exoskeleton. In other words, an insect wears its skeleton outside its body.

Nearly one million kinds of insects have been discovered. Beetles, butterflies, and bees are all insects.

The word insect means "in sections." Look at the picture of the ant. Find the three body sections. Count the legs. An insect always has six legs. The legs are attached to the middle section, or thorax. Some insects have wings too.

Most insects develop in four steps. The first is the egg. Then a larva hatches from the egg. A caterpillar is the larva of a butterfly. The third step is the pupa stage. At that time, the insect wraps itself in a covering called a cocoon or chrysalis (KRIS-uh-lis). Hidden inside, the insect goes through great changes. Finally, the insect cracks open the cocoon and crawls out as an adult.

Ant

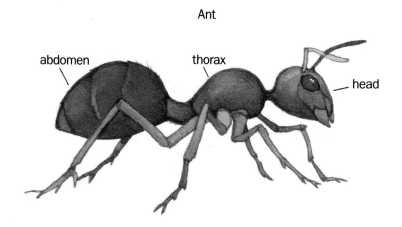

abdomen   thorax   head

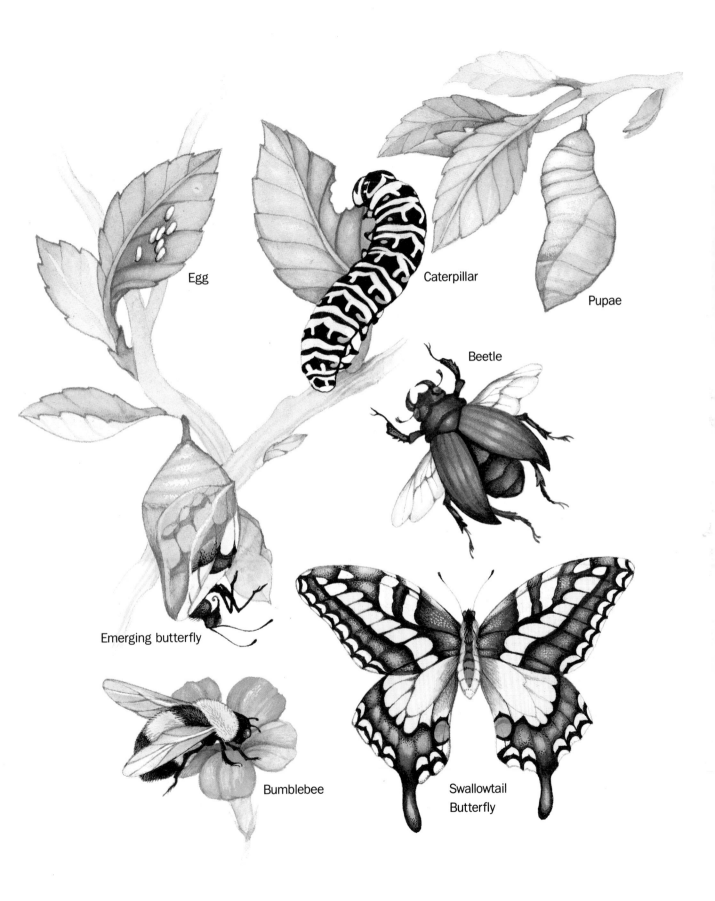

Egg

Caterpillar

Pupae

Beetle

Emerging butterfly

Bumblebee

Swallowtail
Butterfly

MAMMALS

Mammals have backbones and are warm-blooded. This means their body temperature stays the same in hot or cold weather. They breathe air with lungs. Most are covered with hair or fur. Some sea mammals, such as whales, have only a few hairs on the lips, or none at all.

Most female mammals carry their developing babies inside their bodies. A mammal's baby is completely formed when it is born. Females have milk glands to feed their young. A few mammals, like the duck-billed platypus, lay eggs.

Mammals move in many different ways. And they live in many different kinds of places. Seals swim through icy polar water. Camels travel for days through hot, dry deserts. Whales and dolphins swim in warm and cold oceans. And bats fly in the air. Humans are mammals too. So mammals have even walked on the moon!

Human

Rabbits

Camel

Kangaroo

Horse

Seal

Platypus

Bat

Humpback Whale

Dolphins

REPTILES

Dinosaurs, the biggest animals that ever lived, were reptiles. Today there are no dinosaurs. But there are other reptiles. Turtles, lizards, snakes, and alligators are all reptiles.

A reptile has a backbone. And it is cold-blooded. Its body becomes the temperature of the water or air around it. On a hot day a reptile looks for a cooler, shady spot. It may burrow in the sand or swim in a cold river. On a cool day, a reptile may take a warm sunbath.

Most reptiles lay eggs. The sun's heat makes the eggs hatch.

Reptiles breathe air with lungs. Their bodies are usually covered with scales or hard plates. Many reptiles have claws on their toes. Which of the reptiles in the pictures don't have claws? Which don't even have toes?

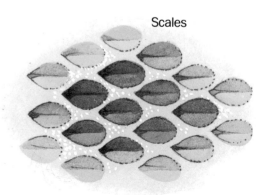

Scales

Turtle Scutes

Dienonychus (a kind of Allosaurus)

Common Pond Turtle

Cobra

Tuatara

Lizard

Alligator in sun

Snake seeking shade

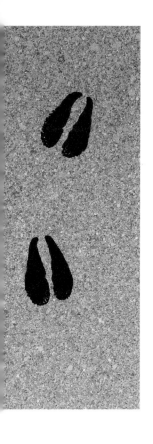

ANTELOPE

CLASS: mammal

HABITAT: grasslands of Africa and Asia

DIET: leaves, twigs, grass

DEFENSE: runs away

TOP SPEED: 60 miles per hour

FOOTNOTES: Antelopes stand on hard hoofs that are divided into two toes. Some antelopes balance on rocky hills by walking on the very tips of their narrow hoofs. Others can jump ten feet high! The antelope in the picture is an impala. It can leap 30 feet when it wants to make a quick get-away.

BABOON

CLASS: mammal

HABITAT: grasslands and seashore cliffs of Africa

DIET: eggs, fruit, grass, insects, leaves, roots

DEFENSE: sharp teeth, gruff bark

TOP SPEED: walks about 5 miles per hour

FOOTNOTES: A baboon walks on its hands and feet. Look at its footprints. Count its fingers and toes. How are they like your own? Baboons live in groups. They use their hands to comb dirt and insects from one another's fur. Baboons travel up to six miles a day, searching for food. The picture shows an olive baboon.

BEAR

CLASS:	mammal
HABITAT:	forests and woodlands of North and South America, Asia, Europe, and the Arctic
DIET:	roots, ants, meat, fish, eggs, honey, fruit
DEFENSE:	sharp teeth and claws
TOP SPEED:	30 miles per hour

FOOTNOTES: Bears have big feet and short legs. Notice the large claws in the footprints. How could those claws help a bear get ants and honey? Bears and people move differently from most other animals. They walk flat on their feet, not up on their toes. The picture shows an American black bear.

BEAVER

CLASS:	mammal
HABITAT:	streams, riverbanks, and lake shores of North America, Asia, and Europe
DIET:	bark, twigs, leaves, roots
DEFENSE:	sharp sense of hearing and smell; swims away
TOP SPEED:	swims about 6 miles per hour

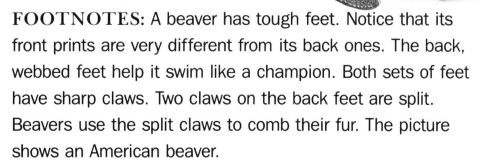

FOOTNOTES: A beaver has tough feet. Notice that its front prints are very different from its back ones. The back, webbed feet help it swim like a champion. Both sets of feet have sharp claws. Two claws on the back feet are split. Beavers use the split claws to comb their fur. The picture shows an American beaver.

BOBCAT

CLASS:	mammal
HABITAT:	woodlands and deserts of North America
DIET:	rabbits, squirrels, gophers, chickens
DEFENSE:	sharp teeth and claws; climbs trees
TOP SPEED:	30 miles per hour

FOOTNOTES: Bobcats use sharp claws to help them climb trees or cactus plants. Even prickly cactus spines don't seem to bother these wild cats. Look at its footprints. Can the bobcat pull its claws back under its skin?

CAT

CLASS:	mammal
HABITAT:	wherever humans live
DIET:	meat, eggs, fish, vegetables, milk, cheese
DEFENSE:	sharp teeth and claws
TOP SPEED:	30 miles per hour

FOOTNOTES: Cats have five toes on each front paw, counting a dewclaw that is higher on the leg. They have four toes on each back paw. All 18 toes have hooked claws. The cat can pull the claws back under its skin. Spongy foot pads help cats sneak up on animals during hunting. When cats fall, they almost always land on their feet! The picture shows a tabby cat.

CHEETAH

CLASS:	mammal
HABITAT:	grasslands of Africa and Asia
DIET:	small animals, antelope, gazelles
DEFENSE:	sharp teeth and claws; runs away
TOP SPEED:	70 miles per hour

FOOTNOTES: Cheetahs are the fastest land animals on earth. They are sleek running machines with long, strong legs. The cheetah is the only cat that cannot pull its claws back under its skin. The claws are always out, ready to hunt or protect. Compare the cheetah's footprints with the leopard's and cat's. Can you spot the cheetah's claws?

COW

CLASS:	mammal
HABITAT:	farms on every continent except Antarctica
DIET:	grass, corn, clover, alfalfa, molasses
DEFENSE:	horns; walks away
TOP SPEED:	usually very slow-moving; may run for a few seconds

FOOTNOTES: A cow is the adult female of animals called cattle. Its hard hoofs are split in two and cover its toes. The hoofs protect the animal's feet and keep it from slipping. Cows raised for milk usually have one baby each spring. The baby is called a calf. It can stand on its feet when it is only 15 minutes old. The cow in the picture is a Holstein.

COYOTE

CLASS:	mammal
HABITAT:	woodlands and plains of central and North America
DIET:	rabbits, gophers, mice, rats, squirrels, antelope, goats, sheep, insects, reptiles, berries, watermelons
DEFENSE:	sharp teeth and claws
TOP SPEED:	about 40 miles per hour

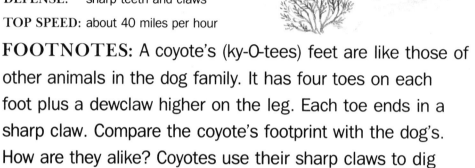

FOOTNOTES: A coyote's (ky-O-tees) feet are like those of other animals in the dog family. It has four toes on each foot plus a dewclaw higher on the leg. Each toe ends in a sharp claw. Compare the coyote's footprint with the dog's. How are they alike? Coyotes use their sharp claws to dig holes called burrows. Their pups are born in the burrows.

DEER

CLASS:	mammal
HABITAT:	forests and woodlands of every continent except Antarctica
DIET:	leaves, acorns, bark, twigs, moss
DEFENSE:	protective coloring; runs away, hides
TOP SPEED:	about 50 miles per hour

FOOTNOTES: Deer run on tiptoe. Look at their footprints. Notice their feet are made of two middle toes. The dots in the footprints are made by dewclaws higher on the deer's leg. You can see dewclaw footprints only in snow or mud. The picture shows a white-tailed deer.

DOG

CLASS:	mammal
HABITAT:	wherever humans live
DIET:	meat, bones, cereal, cheese
DEFENSE:	sharp teeth and claws, loud bark
TOP SPEED:	40 miles per hour

FOOTNOTES: Dogs have four toes on each foot plus a dewclaw higher on each leg. Do the dewclaws show in the footprints? The bottoms of dogs' paws are cushioned with pads of tough skin. The large dog in the picture is a Great Dane. The small dog is a Yorkshire terrier.

DUCK

CLASS:	bird
HABITAT:	lakes and ponds of every continent except Antarctica
DIET:	plants, roots, seeds, snails, insects, fish
DEFENSE:	swims or flies away
TOP SPEED:	flies up to 70 miles per hour

FOOTNOTES: Ducks waddle on land. But their thin legs and webbed feet paddle smoothly in the water. Webbing is skin that holds the toes together. Webbed feet help a duck push water back. And pushing the water back moves the duck forward. The ducks in the picture are male and female mallards. The male has a green head.

ELEPHANT

CLASS: mammal

HABITAT: forest and grasslands of Africa and Asia

DIET: grass, leaves, roots, bark, branches, berries, coconuts, corn, dates, plums, sugar cane

DEFENSE: giant size, thick skin, sharp tusks

TOP SPEED: 25 miles per hour

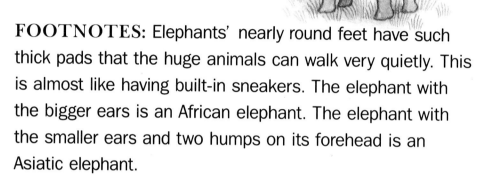

FOOTNOTES: Elephants' nearly round feet have such thick pads that the huge animals can walk very quietly. This is almost like having built-in sneakers. The elephant with the bigger ears is an African elephant. The elephant with the smaller ears and two humps on its forehead is an Asiatic elephant.

FROG

CLASS: amphibian

HABITAT: ponds, rivers, lakes, and streams of every continent except Antarctica

DIET: insects, worms, minnows, spiders

DEFENSE: jumps away; some release poison

TOP SPEED: jumps 20-40 feet in a few seconds

FOOTNOTES: Most frogs have strong back legs that let them jump great distances. Smaller front legs help them balance and land. Many frogs have webbed toes on their hind feet for swimming. Some frogs have sticky toe pads that help them climb trees. The frog in the picture is a bullfrog.

GILA MONSTER

CLASS: reptile

HABITAT: deserts of North America

DIET: bird and reptile eggs, small animals, insects

DEFENSE: poisonous bite

TOP SPEED: less than one mile per hour

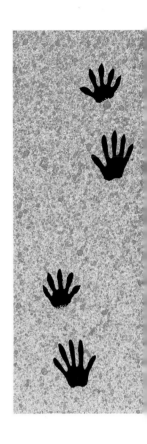

FOOTNOTES: A Gila (HEE-la) monster's legs stick straight out from its body. This makes it hard to travel fast. You may want to get down on your hands and feet and try walking this way. It's not easy!

GIRAFFE

CLASS: mammal

HABITAT: grasslands of Africa

DIET: leaves, twigs, fruit

DEFENSE: protective coloring; runs away, kicks

TOP SPEED: 30 miles per hour

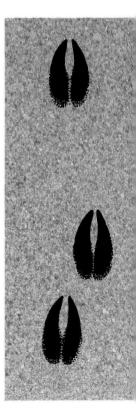

FOOTNOTES: A giraffe's hoofs are split into two parts. Each part is the hardened tip of a toe. A giraffe usually sleeps standing up. It is instantly ready to run from danger. A giraffe's legs are about six feet long. Its neck may be even longer. So it's no surprise that the giraffe is the tallest animal in the world!

GOAT

CLASS:	mammal
HABITAT:	farms on every continent except Antarctica
DIET:	leaves, grass, corn, oats
DEFENSE:	sharp horns
TOP SPEED:	quick for short distances

FOOTNOTES: Goats have hoofs that are split into two toes. The narrow hoofs of some goats help them run up steep mountains. The shaggier goat in the picture is an angora. Its long coat is cut for wool. The other goat is a Toggenburg. It is raised for its milk.

HARE

CLASS:	mammal
HABITAT:	grasslands and deserts of North and Central America, Europe, Asia, Africa, Australia
DIET:	plants
DEFENSE:	sharp sense of hearing; runs away, hides
TOP SPEED:	45 miles per hour

FOOTNOTES: Hares use their long, powerful back legs to jump long distances. Their front legs help them balance. The hare is a close relative of the rabbit. Unlike rabbits, hares are born with their eyes open and with a coat of soft fur. The picture shows a jackrabbit, which is really a hare.

HEN

CLASS: bird

HABITAT: farms on every continent except Antarctica

DIET: grain, seed

DEFENSE: sharp beak and claws

TOP SPEED: 9 miles per hour

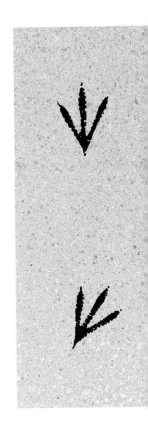

FOOTNOTES: The hen is an adult female chicken. It can lay more than 200 eggs a year. Most chickens have four toes on each foot. Hens would rather walk than fly. Their bodies are heavy and hard to lift off the ground. The picture shows a white leghorn and a brown leghorn hen. Which is which?

HORSE

CLASS: mammal

HABITAT: farms on every continent except Antarctica

DIET: grass, grain, hay

DEFENSE: kicks, bites

TOP SPEED: 45 miles per hour

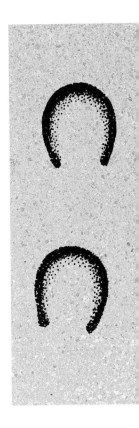

FOOTNOTES: Horses walk on the tips of toes covered by hard hoofs. The rubbery soles of their feet are called frogs. Frogs cushion the feet and legs like thick, bouncy running shoes. Metal horseshoes protect their feet on hard ground. Look at the footprints. Is this horse wearing shoes? The white horse above is a draft horse. The other horse is a Morgan.

JACKAL

CLASS:	mammal
HABITAT:	grasslands of Africa and Asia
DIET:	mice, lizards, insects
DEFENSE:	sharp teeth and claws
TOP SPEED:	35 miles per hour

FOOTNOTES: The jackal is a member of the dog family. Compare the footprints of the dog and the jackal. What is the biggest difference you see? Which animal could use its feet to defend itself better?

KANGAROO RAT

CLASS:	mammal
HABITAT:	plains and deserts of North America
DIET:	seeds, grass, roots
DEFENSE:	sharp teeth; kicks
TOP SPEED:	exact speed unknown

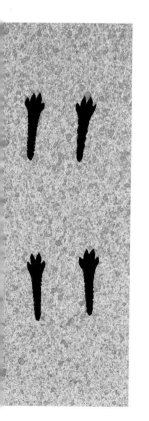

FOOTNOTES: The kangaroo rat's tail is often longer than its head and body together. It uses this tail for balance, hopping from place to place like a kangaroo. This rat uses its tiny front feet to gather food. Its back legs are long like stilts. They help the animal spring up in great leaps. The picture shows Ord's kangaroo rat.

LEOPARD

CLASS: mammal

HABITAT: grasslands and forests of Africa and Asia

DIET: small animals

DEFENSE: sharp teeth and claws

TOP SPEED: about 35 miles per hour

FOOTNOTES: The leopard has spongy foot pads and hooked claws. It keeps the claws under its skin until they are needed. Compare the footprints of the leopard and the cheetah. What is the biggest difference? Leopards use their claws to climb trees, carrying their food with their teeth.

LION

CLASS: mammal

HABITAT: grasslands of Africa, Gir forest of India

DIET: animals with hoofs, fish, turtles, chickens

DEFENSE: sharp teeth and claws

TOP SPEED: 35 miles per hour

FOOTNOTES: A lion's paws can tear an animal apart in one swoop. Lions hold their claws back most of the time to keep them sharp. In the picture, the lion with the shaggy mane is a male. The furry collar helps him look even bigger than he is. The lion without the mane is a female.

OSTRICH

CLASS:	bird
HABITAT:	grasslands of Africa
DIET:	plants, lizards, turtles
DEFENSE:	kicks
TOP SPEED:	40 miles per hour

FOOTNOTES: The ostrich is the biggest bird on earth. It has wings but cannot fly. It escapes from enemies by running away on its powerful legs. The ostrich is the only bird with two toes on each foot. The ostrich with the handsome black and white feathers is a male. The bird with the dull brown feathers is a female. Why might it be better to have dull feathers?

OWL

CLASS:	bird
HABITAT:	woodlands of North America, Europe, Asia, Australia
DIET:	rabbits, squirrels, mice, rats, birds, insects, fish
DEFENSE:	protective coloring, good night vision, sharp claws
TOP SPEED:	40 miles per hour

FOOTNOTES: Its feathers are so fluffy that an owl makes almost no noise as it flies. Owls use their sharp claws to capture dinner. The owl in the picture is a great horned owl. Bunches of feathers on its head look like horns. But don't let them fool you.

PIG

CLASS: mammal

HABITAT: farms on every continent except Antarctica

DIET: corn, alfalfa, oats, peanuts, meat scraps

DEFENSE: sharp teeth; runs away

TOP SPEED: 11 miles per hour

FOOTNOTES: Pigs are the smartest of all farm animals. They can learn to roll over and to fetch things. Pigs have four toes that end in a hard hoof on each foot. What are the two dots in each footprint? If you need help, read the section about deer. In the picture, the pig in front is a Landrace. The other one is a Hampshire.

PRAIRIE DOG

CLASS: mammal

HABITAT: prairies and plains of North America

DIET: grass, grains, alfalfa, insects

DEFENSE: sharp teeth and claws, noisy bark; runs away

TOP SPEED: exact speed unknown; probably about 15 miles per hour

FOOTNOTES: Prairie dogs use their feet and claws to dig burrows in the earth. These holes usually have sleeping and food storage rooms. Homes of different prairie dogs often connect, forming large towns. Prairie dogs bark warnings to each other when there is danger. The picture shows a black-tailed prairie dog.

RABBIT

CLASS:	mammal
HABITAT:	woodlands and meadows of North and Central America, Europe, Africa, and Australia
DIET:	leaves, clover, grass, weeds, twigs, fruit, vegetables
DEFENSE:	sharp sense of hearing, protective coloring; runs away, sits still
TOP SPEED:	18 miles per hour

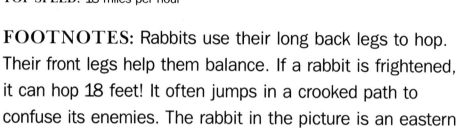

FOOTNOTES: Rabbits use their long back legs to hop. Their front legs help them balance. If a rabbit is frightened, it can hop 18 feet! It often jumps in a crooked path to confuse its enemies. The rabbit in the picture is an eastern cottontail.

RACCOON

CLASS:	mammal
HABITAT:	woodlands of North and Central America
DIET:	grain, seeds, leaves, acorns, eggs, fruit, fish, frogs, grasshoppers, mice, meat
DEFENSE:	sharp teeth and claws
TOP SPEED:	15 miles per hour

FOOTNOTES: The raccoon's sharp claws help it climb trees and catch food. It uses its hand-like front paws to hold things. And it swims well too! Raccoons walk flat on the ground with all four feet. What other animal's prints show that it walks this way? The picture shows a North American raccoon.

RATTLESNAKE

CLASS: reptile

HABITAT: plains, mountains, and deserts of North and South America

DIET: insects, birds, mice, rats, other small animals

DEFENSE: poisonous bite, rattle noise

TOP SPEED: 2 miles per hour

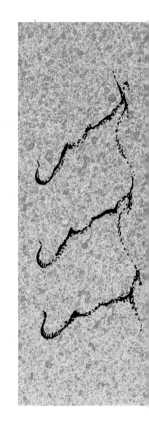

FOOTNOTES: Snakes have no feet at all. They slither across the ground on their bellies. The rattlesnake has about 200 joints in its long backbone to help it move. It is named for the rattle at the end of its tail. The rattle is made of dry rings of skin. Its sound frightens enemies away. The picture shows a western diamondback.

RED FOX

CLASS: mammal

HABITAT: forests and fields of North America, Asia, and Europe

DIET: fruit, mice, rats, birds, fish

DEFENSE: sharp teeth and claws

TOP SPEED: 40 miles per hour

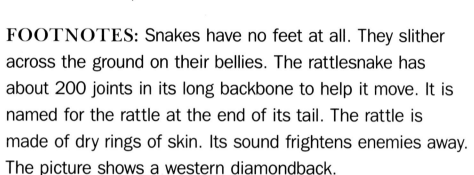

FOOTNOTES: The red fox is part of the dog family. Compare its footprints to those of the coyote and the dog. When a fox walks, its back feet step right into the footprints made by its front ones. This is not true when it runs. Look at the footprints. Notice the separate front and back prints. Is this fox walking?

ROADRUNNER

CLASS:	bird
HABITAT:	deserts of North America
DIET:	insects, baby birds, gophers, mice, lizards, snakes
DEFENSE:	sharp beak; runs quickly
TOP SPEED:	runs up to 15 miles per hour

FOOTNOTES: Roadrunners can fly. But they'd much rather run along the ground. They seem to like running down roads, then racing to safety as cars get close. The roadrunner is a member of the cuckoo family.

ROOSTER

CLASS:	bird
HABITAT:	farms of every continent except Antarctica
DIET:	grain, seeds
DEFENSE:	sharp spurs (spikes) on its legs
TOP SPEED:	9 miles per hour

FOOTNOTES: The rooster is a male chicken. Most roosters have four toes. The rooster has wings, but it doesn't fly well. The picture shows a white leghorn and a brown leghorn rooster. Compare them to the hens shown on page 27. How are they the same? How are they different?

SHEEP

CLASS: mammal

HABITAT: farms of every continent except Antarctica

DIET: grass, grain, hay

DEFENSE: runs away; some have sharp horns

TOP SPEED: quick for short distances

FOOTNOTES: Sheep's feet are divided into two toes. Their thick, strong thighs help them move quickly. Sheep and goats are alike in some ways. Look at the goat's footprints on page 26. How are they like the sheep's prints? How are they different? Merino and Suffolk sheep are shown. The Merino is prized for its long woolly coat.

SKUNK

CLASS: mammal

HABITAT: North and South America

DIET: caterpillars, crickets, beetles, mice, rats, eggs, fruit, grain

DEFENSE: terrible smell

TOP SPEED: 4 miles per hour

FOOTNOTES: A skunk has very few enemies. Once you have smelled one, it is easy to understand why. First the skunk stamps its front feet. It also clicks its tongue as a warning. If that doesn't work, the skunk raises itself on its front legs. Then it shoots a smelly liquid at its enemy. The picture shows a striped skunk.

TORTOISE

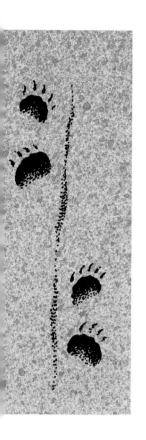

CLASS: reptile

HABITAT: deserts, forests, grasslands, swamps of North and South America, Africa, Asia, and Europe

DIET: grass, leaves, small animals

DEFENSE: hides in shell, bites with hard beak

TOP SPEED: less than one mile per hour

FOOTNOTES: Most turtles live in water. But tortoises live on land. They use their strong front legs to dig burrows in the sand. Tortoises hide from the sun and sleep in these holes. The tortoise above is a desert tortoise. It eats only plants.

VULTURE

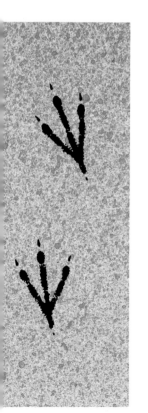

CLASS: bird

HABITAT: deserts and open plains of North and South America, Europe, Africa, and Asia

DIET: dead animals

DEFENSE: flies away

TOP SPEED: up to 89 miles per hour

FOOTNOTES: Vultures are ugly birds with no feathers on their heads. But they fly gracefully in wide, high circles. They have weak beaks and dull claws. So they can carry only weak or dead animals to eat. The vulture in the picture is a turkey vulture.

WOODPECKER

CLASS: bird

HABITAT: forests of North and South America, Europe, Asia, and Africa

DIET: insects, fruits, nuts

DEFENSE: flies away

TOP SPEED: exact speed unknown

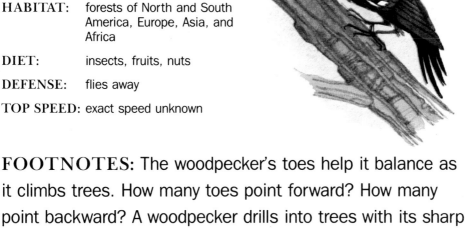

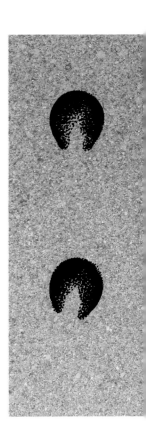

FOOTNOTES: The woodpecker's toes help it balance as it climbs trees. How many toes point forward? How many point backward? A woodpecker drills into trees with its sharp beak. A long, sticky tongue gathers its insect lunch. The picture shows a pileated (PY-lee-ay-tid) or capped woodpecker.

ZEBRA

CLASS: mammal

HABITAT: grasslands of Africa

DIET: grass

DEFENSE: protective coloring; kicks, bites

TOP SPEED: 40 miles per hour

FOOTNOTES: Zebras belong to the horse family. But they are harder to train than horses. Compare the footprints of the horse and the zebra. How are they similar? The stripes of every single zebra are different. The zebra in the picture is a Burchell's zebra.

1. A desert animal is hidden in this picture. Follow nature's footprints to find the animal. Which animal is it?

2. An African grasslands animal is hidden in this picture. Follow nature's footprints to find the animal. Which animal is it?

3. A woodlands animal is hidden in this picture. Follow
nature's footprints to find the animal. Which animal is it?

4. A barnyard animal is hidden in this picture. Follow
nature's footprints to find the animal. Which animal is it?

1.

3.

2.

4.